Jesus' New Believer's Handbook

Starting the Christian Journey

Written and Illustrated by
J. Niki

All Scripture quotations are from the King James Version of the Holy Bible.

Jesus' New Believer's Handbook – Starting the Christian Journey

Conditions of Use

Permission is hereby granted to copy and use any single poem, except on web sites, by an individual, by churches, hospitals, and funeral homes as long as credit is given to the author. The poems, pictures, and images may not be used on web sites. Any and all commercial use of poems or pictures is reserved by J.Niki Enterprises, LLC. Permission to use poems, pictures, and images otherwise, must be obtained in writing from J. Niki, Enterprises, LLC.

Copyright © February 2016 by J. Nik Enterprises. LLC
All rights reserved.

J. Niki Enterprises, LLC
1850 Cotillion Drive
Suite 2209
Atlanta, Georgia 30338

Library of Congress Cataloging-in Publication Data

ISBN 978-0-979-0442-4-3
ISBN 0-9790442-4-3

Introduction

Jesus spent three years with His disciples teaching them and allowing them to experience life in His presence. They experienced faith in Jesus lived out before them every day. He was their Teacher and Mentor. They asked questions and received answers. Then, they went out into the world, and using what they had learned, grew in spirit and faith accomplishing miracles for Jesus's kingdom to come and leaving us the second half of the Holy Bible, The New Testament, to live by.

This little volume has been written for New Believers who may or may not have a mentor as they start their Christian journey. I have tried to balance the thoughts to meet the needs of children, teens, and adults alike, because New Believers come in all ages. It is meant to be a companion to your Bible as you start your daily walk with the Lord. If you will read the Biblical references in the footnotes, you will begin to navigate through the different Books of the Bible and to develop "eyes to see and ears to hear." [1]

This Handbook offers a "wheelhouse," or shelter, as you travel the life of God's purpose along the narrow path. It contains navigational tools to assist you around and through the trials and pitfalls the devil will place in your way. Don't stress. Everybody has trials and temptation. You just need to learn the way to successfully pass through them.

Always remember, if you have accepted Jesus, you are a child of God, an heir with Jesus in His eternal kingdom. No one can take your salvation away. Your name is written in the Lamb's Book of Life and it can never be erased.

God has a purpose for you. To accomplish it, Jesus is always with you. The Holy Spirit will lead and guide you. "Be strong and of good courage… be not afraid..." [2] as you live the remainder of your life serving the Lord as a student, parent, professional, skilled or creative artisan. In all you do, keep your eyes on Jesus. He will never leave you.

[1] Matthew 13:16.   [2] Joshua 1:9.

J. Niki

Dedication

To my sister, for whom I thank God every day; my closest prayer partner, the first-line editor of each of my books, and my precious friend.

Although we have journeyed in different directions in our adult life, yet we are bonded in faith, upbringing, trials, and cherished adventures. Together, we cannot make a pot of coffee without making a mess, but we have seen a multitude of shared prayers answered in blessings, and we joyfully proclaim the Truth of Jesus Christ and the Word of God.

Table of Contents

Paul's Prayer for Believers	1
My Prayer	3
Who is Jesus?	4
What is Salvation?	7
A Prayer for Salvation	9
Record of Your Salvation	10
What it Means to be a Christian	11
Profession of Belief in Jesus	12
Choosing a Church	13
Public Profession of Belief in Jesus	14
Church Membership	16
Record of Your First Church Membership	17
What is a Church Ordinance?	18
The Ordinance of Baptism	20
Record of Your Baptism	21
The Lord's Supper (Communion)	22
The Ordinance of Communion	24
Record of Your First Communion	25
How Do You Pray?	26
The Lord's Prayer	27

Table of Contents, *continued*

Developing Prayer Patterns	28
The A.C.T.S. of Prayer	29
Quality Prayer	31
Record of Quality Prayer: Time and Place	34
The Holy Bible	35
The Bible...The Scripture ...The Word of God	36
Choosing a Holy Bible	38
The Ten Commandments	39
The First and Greatest Commandment	40
Scriptures to Live By	41
The Great Commission	44
The Whole Armor of God	46
Singing Hymns and Gospel Songs	48
The J.O.Y. of Life	50
God Will Lead You	51
Progressing on Your Christian Journey	52

Paul's Prayer for Believers
Colossians 1: 9-14

⁹ For this cause we also, since the day we heard it, do not cease to pray for you, and to desire that ye might be filled with the knowledge of his will in all wisdom and spiritual understanding;

¹⁰ That ye might walk worthy of the Lord unto all pleasing, being fruitful in every good work, and increasing in the knowledge of God;

¹¹ Strengthened with all might, according to his glorious power, unto all patience and longsuffering with joyfulness;

¹² Giving thanks unto the Father, which hath made us meet to be partakers of the inheritance of the saints in light:

¹³ Who hath delivered us from the power of darkness, and hath translated us into the kingdom of his dear Son."

¹⁴ In whom we have redemption through his blood, even the forgiveness of sins.

"My Prayer"

Lord,[1] for all Jesus' New Believers,
I praise and glorify Your name.
May they grow in faith and spirit,
Serving You, their focused aim.

Father, take these teaching verses ...
May they bless the heart that reads;
May they be a godly influence
To meet New Believers' needs.

These are the words You've given ...
Fashioned as my heart's almsdeeds;[2]
May they carry Your authority
As they become Your Gospel seeds.
Amen.

---

[1] "Lord" refers to God: the Father, Jesus, and the Holy Spirit. They all hear when you pray "Lord."
[2] Gifts of love.

Who is Jesus?

Jesus is the Son of God ...
With God at the Creation.
With the Holy Spirit, Three in One…
The Triune[1] God offers man salvation.[2]

They made man in their image[3]
For a personal relationship,
But Adam's disobedience
Brought sin and broke their fellowship.[4]

Sin, man's innate,[5] fleshly nature,[6]
Carries a price we all must pay:[7]
Eternal pain ... gnashing of teeth ...
When we face the Judgment Day.[8]

But God so loved His creation,
That He sent His only Son
Into the world to bring salvation;[9]
To repair what sin had done.

If you believe The Holy Bible…
Believe that Jesus was God's Son…
Believe He died … was resurrected…
That is faith! Your journey has begun.[10]

---

[1] Triune: **Elohim** (Hebrew) the Trinity; plural noun for God with singular meaning when it refers to the One True Living God.
[2] Romans 10:9-10.
[3] Genesis 1:26.
[4] Genesis 3.
[5] Inherent; inseparable.
[6] Romans 3:23.
[7] Romans 6:23.
[8] Romans 1:16-18.
[9] To save us from sin.
[10] II Corinthians 5:7.

What is Salvation?

Before we start Believer's training,
We should recall where we've all been...
Before we met the One True Savior,
And Jesus took away our sin.

We have from birth, a sinful nature;
It often leads us to do wrong.
It is directed by the devil.
It is wicked. It is strong.

We were on the road of Satan:
"Perdition" -- Hell -- it's rightful name.
Death to our spirit: ... ruination ...
Is Satan's goal; his only aim.

But then, one day the Holy Spirit,
Drew us to God ... opened our eyes:
We were sinners -- worldly orphans --
Doomed for hell, we realized.

Confessing sin, asking forgiveness,
Repenting,[1] in the Savior's name;
We cried out for God to save us,
By His grace,[2] from sin and shame.

With His precious blood, Christ saved us[3] --
Willingly, laid down His life --
Showed us love -- no other greater --
Gifted us eternal life.

We became a new creation[4]
When Jesus took away our sin.
Then God sealed us with His Spirit...[5]
New life in Jesus...we were born again![6]

[1] Turning away from sin.
[2] Ephesians 2:8.
[3] I Peter 1:19-21.
[4] II Corinthians 5:17.
[5] II Corinthians 1:22.
[6] Rebirth: accepting Jesus Christ as your Savior (John 3:3&7).

A Prayer for Salvation

Lord, all of my sin I lay at the cross.
Forgive me, Oh God, I know Christ paid sin's cost.
I believe that Christ Jesus was Your only Son,
Through His resurrection, my salvation was won.
I trust in Your Word; I come humbly to You;
Forgive all my sins; let my life start anew.
Come into my heart and make it Your own;
Make a change in my life; never leave me alone.
Help me to read the Scripture each day;
Show me Your purpose; please light my way.

Jesus' New Believer's Handbook – J. Niki

RECORD OF YOUR SALVATION

Name: _____

Date of salvation (re-birth: when you accepted Jesus)

_____ Age: _____

Event that drew you to the Lord: _____

_____

_____

_____

_____

_____

_____

_____

Who prayed salvation's prayer with you? _____

_____

What it Means to be a Christian

When you accepted Jesus Christ,
Asking Him into your heart,
You became a New Believer -
Of God's family, you're a part.
Now you have a Christian heritage
Beyond the annals[1] man can search;
A family where Christ is the bridegroom,
You are His bride: part of His Church.[2]

The only way to be a Christian
Is to believe in Jesus Christ…
The Son of God…born of a virgin…
Died on a cross… Christ paid sin's price.[3]
Rose from the dead: was resurrected
On the third day, from the grave.
For forty days, He walked among men[4]…
Living proof He'd come to save.
He ascended back to heaven...
At God's right hand, He sits today[5]…
Interceding[6] … speaking for us…
Because we sin along our way.

---

[1] Records of history.
[2] The Church: one body in Christ (Romans 12:5).
[3] I John 4:10.
[4] Acts 1:3.
[5] Hebrews 12:2.
[6] I John 2:1.

Profession[1] of Belief in Jesus

When you felt the Savior knocking …
When you knew that you had sinned …
You confessed your sins to Jesus …
Gave Him your life and asked Christ in.

Once you were saved, you longed to tell it.
To spread the news to all you know.
You wanted loved ones to know Jesus...
You started Gospel[2] seeds to sow.

"I've asked Jesus to forgive me;
He has washed my sins away.
I surrendered my life to Him;
Now, I walk the Christian way."

"I have turned from my old habits.
Christ is now in all I do.
Don't you think you'd like to meet Him?
He can be your Savior, too."

---

[1] Speaking one's belief.
[2] Good news.

Choosing A Church

Pray for God to lead and plant you
In a Gospel preaching church;
Where members love and serve His purpose:
For the lost, ne'er fail to search.

Where the minister is faithful,
Preaching from God's Holy Word ...
The congregation echoes, "Amen!"
To the sermon they have heard.

Public Profession of Belief in Jesus

Before the church,[1] make your profession:
Let them know that you've been saved.
Request that you become a member --
You wish to walk the path Christ paved.

Before they welcome and receive you,
You might be asked to take a class:
The doctrine of denomination[1] ...
And to learn the church's past.

Will you support the congregation
With your presence, prayers and means;
With whatever God has given:
Talent, time, as Jesus deems?

Making your profession public
Makes the expectation clear:
You have accepted Christ as Savior.
Let all those present witness...hear.

---

[1] Baptist, Methodist, Presbyterian, Lutheran, and other Protestant faiths ... believe in Jesus as the ONLY WAY TO GOD, but differ in doctrine on non-salvation issues.

Church Membership

When you became a new church member,
You became a vital part
Of the work of Christ's commission,[1]
So, don't hesitate to start.

Make an effort to be present
For Services throughout the week.
Formal worship is inspiring ...
Righteous hearts and minds to keep.

Fellowship is a true blessing
Godly support and use of time;
Companionship with true Believers
Keeps your thoughts and heart sublime.[2]

Lift your church and pastor daily
To the Lord in fervent[3] prayers.
Vital to God's missionaries:
Others pray, support, and care.

Give your tithes[4] and weekly offerings --
First fruits[5] -- with generosity --
Knowing God receives and blesses,
Returning more abundantly.[6]

Be always true to keep your word
First, to the Lord and then, the church.
You are God's child -- a new church member --
Don't leave either in the lurch.[7]

[1] Matthew 28:19-20.
[2] Elevated; exalted.
[3] Ardent; intense (James 5:16).
[4] One-tenth (Genesis 28:22).
[5] First part of income (Exodus 22:29).
[6] Proverbs 3:9-10.
[7] Wanting; in need.

RECORD OF FIRST CHURCH MEMBERSHIP

Church: _____

Location: _____

_____

Pastor: _____

Sunday School Teacher: _____

Youth Minister: _____

What is a Church Ordinance?

The church has many functions:
Worship, fellowship;
Marriages and funerals;
Scriptural scholarship.

There are two Christian ordinances,
Ceremonies Believers celebrate,
Scheduled by their church's leaders,
In which its members participate.

The Ordinance of ***Baptism***
Follows New Believers' faith professions.

Communion, The Lord's Supper,
Reminds us of Christ's dying passions.[1]

---

[1] Suffering.

The Ordinance of Baptism

Christ's death, burial, and resurrection …
Are symbolized when you're baptized.
You identify with Jesus,
Who, for your sins, was crucified.

Baptism is a sign to all,
That you have accepted Jesus;
That you desire to walk His path;
Trust God in all; do as He pleases.

"I baptize you … in the name
Of Father, Son, and Holy Spirit."
Beneath the water, as in death,
Raised … for Christ's Kingdom's credit.

Reborn to throw off fleshly man
And walk in Jesus' righteousness.[1]
Living in God's Holy Word,
You are favored. You are blessed.

---

[1] Godliness.

RECORD OF YOUR BAPTISM

Name: _____

Date of Salvation: _____ Age: _____

Date of Baptism: _____

Baptized by: _____

Location: _____

_____

The Lord's Supper (Communion)

I Corinthians 11:24-26

24 And when he had given thanks, he broke it, and said, Take, eat: this is my body, which is broken for you: this do in remembrance of me.

25 After the same manner also he took the cup, when he had supped, saying, This cup is the new testament in my blood[1]: this do, as often as ye drink it, in remembrance of me.

26 For as often as ye eat this bread, and drink this cup, ye do show the Lord's death till he come.

---

[1] Jesus declared His death would initiate a New Covenant [contract] based on belief in Jesus' death and resurrection. By confession and repentance of sin, everyone, both Jews and Gentiles alike, were offered salvation (John 3:16-17).

The Ordinance of Communion

Communion's not for anyone
Who's not been saved nor been baptized.
It is a sacred, holy remembrance
Of what Jesus sacrificed.

Never take Communion
Without examining your heart.
If there is sin, you've not confessed,
In communion, do not take part.[1]

The Ordinance of Communion,
The Lord's Supper, commemorates
Jesus' body broken; His blood shed.
His death … this remembrance venerates.[2]

**"This bread: ...my body...broken…
Take, eat, in remembrance of me."
This cup: the new testament...my blood …
shed for you…
Drink, ye, in remembrance of me."**

Then sing a song together
Before going on your way ...
Looking up and pondering[3] ...
Christ's return again one day.[4]

---

[1] 1 Corinthians 11:29-30.
[2] Exalts; hallows.
[3] To think deeply upon.
[4] The *Rapture* is written of, but is not named as such (I Thessalonians 4:16-18).

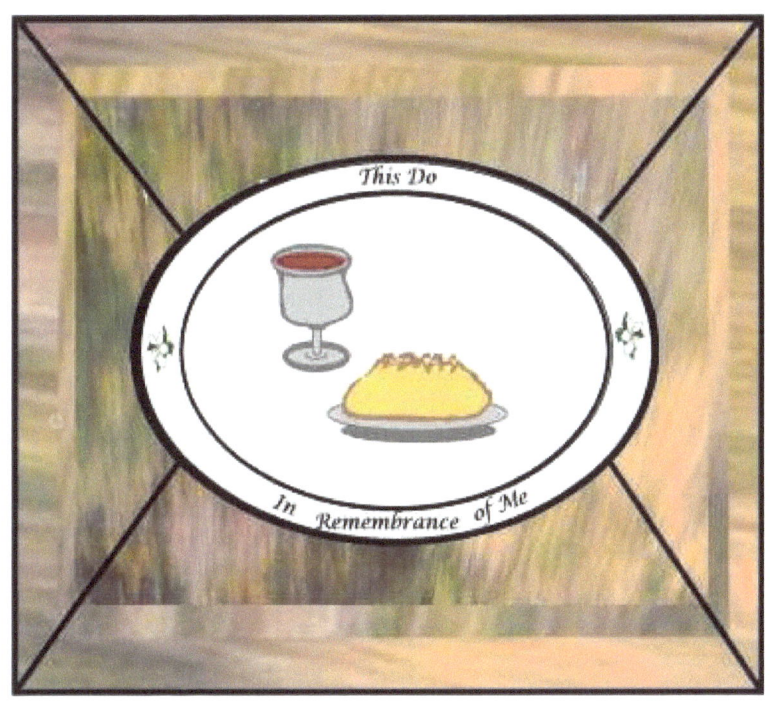

RECORD OF YOUR FIRST COMMUNION

Date: _____ Time: _____

Location: _____

_____

Song: _____

How Do We Pray?

"What is the proper way to pray?"[1]
The disciples asked the Lord one day.
In just a few short phrases,
Jesus taught them what to say.

"Our Father, who art in heaven…"
The Lord's Prayer begins this way.
Simple, reverent, humble…
We seek to meet the Lord each day …
To weave a relationship with God,
In which we're one with Them;[2]
That we may walk and grow in grace,
And that the world grow dim.

The Lord's Prayer is our model
When we come to God in prayer …
When you meet with Christ, our Savior …
Your heart and soul to bare.

---

[1] Luke 11:1-4.
[2] John 17:20-21.

The Lord's Prayer
Matthew 6:9-13

⁹ After this manner, therefore, pray ye: Our Father who art in heaven, Hallowed be thy name.

¹⁰ Thy kingdom come, Thy will be done in earth, as it is in heaven.

¹¹ Give us this day our daily bread.

¹² And forgive us our debts, as we forgive our debtors.

¹³ And lead us not into temptation, but deliver us from evil: For thine is the kingdom, and the power, and the glory, forever. Amen.

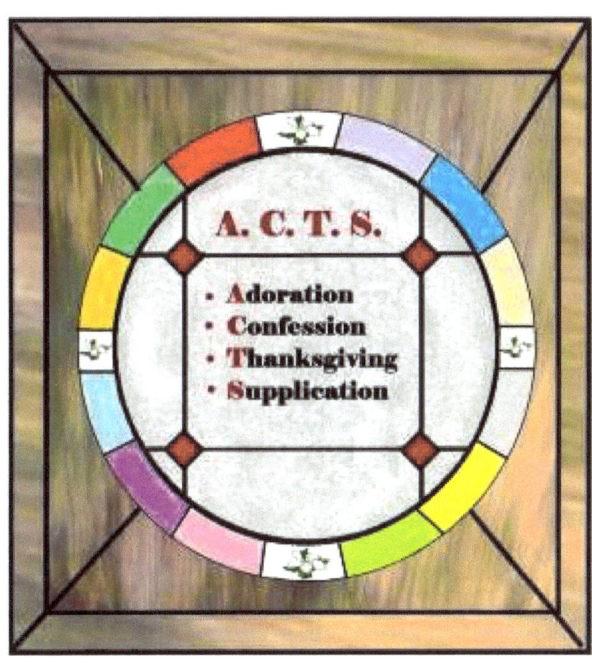

Developing Prayer Patterns

Children learn to pray at bedtime
Before they go to sleep.
Asking God to bless their loved ones,
O'er themselves, His watch to keep.

Children's prayers are so important
To show the Lord respect and love …
To embrace a pattern … emboss a lifestyle …
That honors Christ and God above.

Everyone should pray a blessing…
Giving grace…before each meal:
Thanking God, and asking blessing
On their food … their life … as He should will.

In faithfulness, we develop
Reflex[1] in going straight to prayer
With each trial, each decision …
Knowing God will meet us there.

---

[1] Automatic action.

The A.C.T.S. of Prayer

"A" stands for Adoration:
To acknowledge God, the Omnipotent[1] --
All Knowing, the Creator,
From whom Jesus Christ was sent.

"C" is for Confession:
To ask forgiveness of any sin
That might have been committed
Since last you met with Him.

"T" stands for Thanksgiving:
Praise for the blessings you've received;
For grace and mercy, answered prayers;
For daily sins reprieve.[2]

"S" stands for Supplication:
To lift others' needs before God's throne;
Then for your daily needs … desires --
Place God's will before your own.

Learn from what Christ has taught you:
Always trust God and obey.
Come to God in gratitude
Early and throughout the day.

---

[1] All powerful.   [2] Canceled punishment.

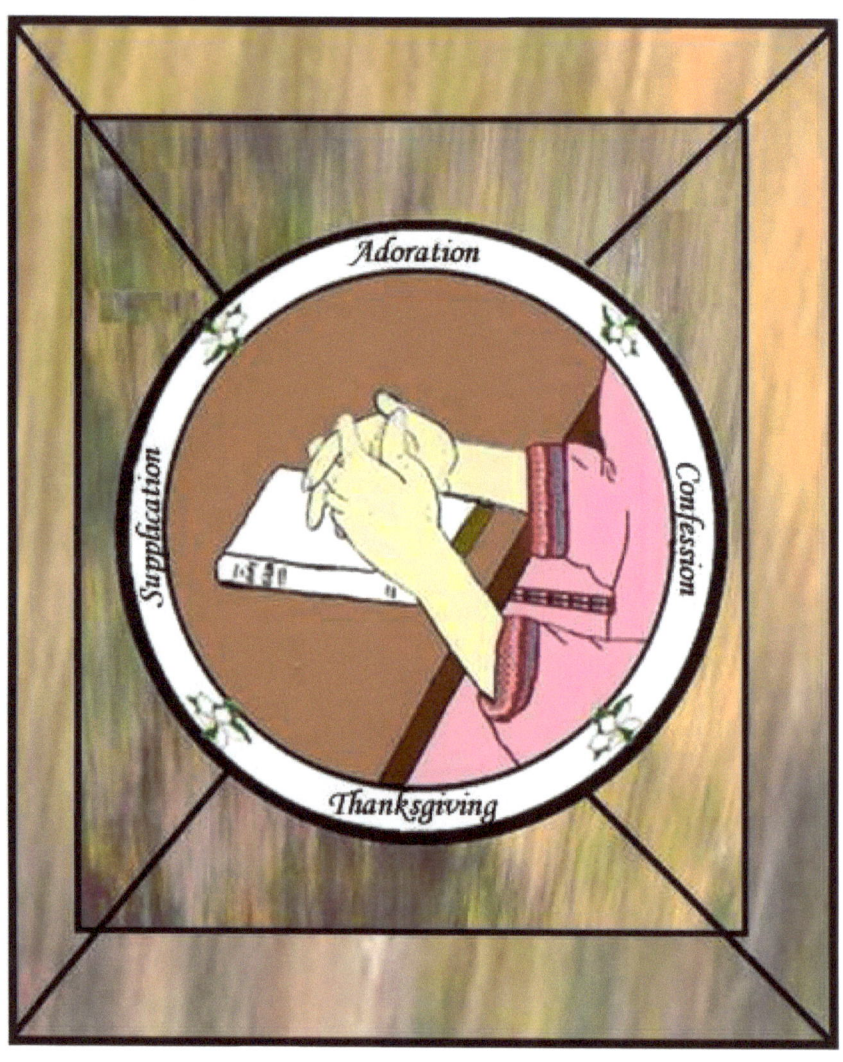

Quality Prayer

Prayer is so exciting!
It is meeting with the Lord --
One-on-One with Jesus --
Two hearts in one accord.

First, ask Him to forgive you[1]
For any sins that you've committed
Since last you met with Him in prayer ...
Insure new sins have been remitted.[2]
For God cannot attend your prayer
If sin comes in between.[3]
Confession is essential
For answers to be seen.[4]

Then tell God of your love and thanks
For blessings He has given;
For saving you and promising
Eternal life with Him in heaven.
Praise Him for His majesty!
For health and financial provision;
For all the things you've needed;
For His help with each decision.

For the Holy Spirit ...
For His comfort and insight;
For sealing you for heaven;
For showing you what's right.

Prayer is the *best gift* you can offer
One you love or one in need.
Lifting others' names to Jesus,
Is blessing God will always heed.[5]
Everyone needs prayer each day,
And God honors the intercessor ...
One who prays in Jesus' name ...
"God's will" ... a faithful praying warrior.

Then in prayer, **just talk to Christ**
About your needs...and what's desired ...
He knows your future and your heart ...
If it's selfish ... or inspired.
Ask for wisdom and direction;
Give Him all you have and will;
He knows best just what to give you ...
Just what blessings to fulfill.

Prayer is such a special gift …
God is near and always true …
There to listen and to answer …
Desiring all His best for you.

But answers come in one of three:
"No, that isn't what is best;"
"Yes, I will do that, My child;" or
"Wait ... in My time, you will be blessed."

Understanding is not promised
For answers you don't like.
God's ways are greater than our own[6]
He is Sovereign;[7] it's His right.

"Pray without ceasing."[8] "How?" you ask.
"That's impossible to do."
"Not if, in your subconscious,
You're conscious Christ is there with you.

Your mind is always working,
Multi-tasking … ev'n in sleep.
You can program prayer and praises,
Scripture there to always keep."

Find a place … a chair … a closet ...
Where you can meet the Lord in prayer ...
A place where you'll not be distracted ...
A time of quality ... to share.
Dedicate this time and place
To meet with your Dear Friend,
For there's no other … sister … brother …
Whose love is faithful and will not end.

Prayer is a cherished intimacy ...
A sweet sound and savor to the Lord…
Neglected … you will live in sorrow …
With losses you cannot afford.

[1] Isaiah 1:18.
[2] Forgiven.
[3] Isaiah 59:2.
[4] I John 1:9.
[5] James 5:15-16.
[6] Isaiah 55:8-11.
[7] Supreme power.
[8] I Thessalonians 5:17.

RECORD OF PRAYER TIME AND PLACE

Dedicated morning prayer time: _____

Dedicated evening prayer time: _____

Dedicated prayer place: _____

_____

The Holy Bible

II Timothy 2:15

[15] **Study to show thyself approved unto God, a workman that needeth not to be ashamed, rightly dividing the word of truth.**

II Timothy 3:16-17

[16] **All scripture is given by inspiration of God, and is profitable for doctrine, for reproof, for correction, for instruction in righteousness:**
[17] **That the man of God may be perfect, thoroughly furnished unto all good works.**

The Bible ... The Scripture... The Word of God

The Bible was inspired by God
Elohim, the Triune God as One --
His character, His attributes --
The Father, Holy Spirit, Son.
God whispered words to at least forty,
Who wrote one cogent[1] eternal work.[2]
Man has a need for salvation ...
Sin has a price man cannot shirk.

The Bible is about **The Word:**
Jesus[3] from Genesis to Revelation:
The history of fallen man ...
Of God's grace and Christ's salvation.

It is the **Holy Spirit**,
Comforter, and Guide,
Who seals man with salvation ...
Who indwells[4] ... in man abides.

The **BIBLE** is our manual:
Believer's **I**nstructions **B**efore **L**eaving **E**arth;
Our MapQuest© and our recipes
For living after our rebirth.

The **Word of God** is medicine
To the lost and wounded soul.
It is comfort. It is healing
For the grieving, young and old.

It is history; adventure;
It is poetry and law;
Biography and prophecy…
Six thousand years of Triune awe!
How can we know of heaven
If we ne'er take the time to learn?
How can we live for Jesus
If we aren't wise and can't discern?

Read your Bible everyday…
Take time to *drink* it in.
It will change to living waters:
Refresh, restore, in time you spend.
Memorize the Scriptures…
Those that hold a special place …
The times you felt God's presence …
Knelt before Him … received His grace.
Keep your Bible at your hand...
Take it with you everywhere...
In your heart, your mind, your soul -
'T will be your strength, protection, care.

The Bible is the precious,
Priceless Word of God…
It is Jesus, our Good Shepherd;
God's living Sword, and guiding Rod.

---

[1] Compelling argument.
[2] Isaiah 40:8.
[3] John 1:1-5.
[4] Be permanently present.

Choosing a Holy Bible

Choose a Bible with concordance,
        references, and index,
Maps, and wider margin pages...
        easy-on-the-eyes-sized text.
The version preference of your pastor,
        I would highly recommend.
But it is Schofield's© King James Bible©
        that is my preference to my end.

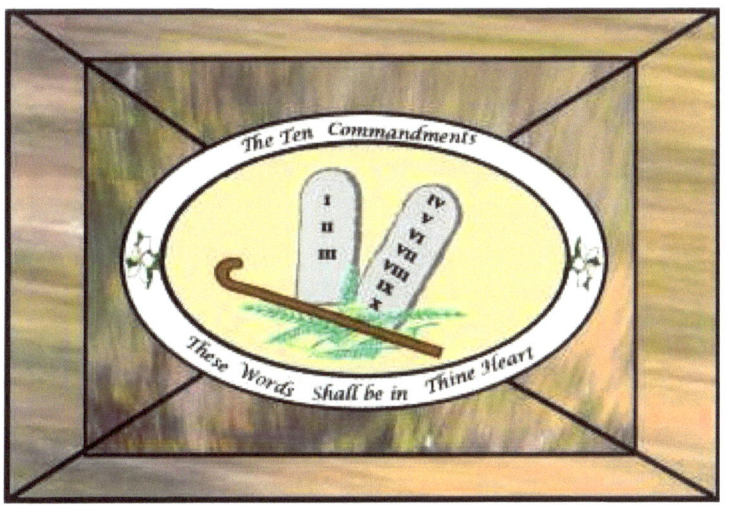

The Ten Commandments[1]

1. "Thou shalt have no other gods before me."
2. "Thou shalt not make unto thee any graven[2] images..."
3. "Thou shalt not take the name of the LORD thy God in vain..."
4. "Remember the Sabbath day, to keep it holy..."
5. "Honor thy father and thy mother...."
6. "Thou shalt not kill."
7. "Thou shalt not commit adultery."
8. "Thou shalt not steal."
9. "Thou shalt not bear false witness..."[3]
10. "Thou shalt not covet[4]..."

---

[1] Exodus 20:3-17.
[2] Carve; shape.
[3] Lie.
[4] Desire what belongs to another.

The First and Greatest Commandment

Mark 12:30-31

³⁰ **And thou shalt love the Lord thy God with all thy heart, and with all thy soul, and with all thy mind, and with all thy strength: this is the first commandment.**
³¹ **And the second is this: Thou shalt love thy neighbour as thyself. There is no other commandment greater than these.**

Ten Commandments Merged to Two[1]

God gave man Ten Commandments
To obey and honor Him;
To live in peace with others,
In righteousness ... Christ's homonym.[2]

**"Love God with all your heart,
your soul, your mind...
Love your neighbor as yourself ..."**
This is God's law divine.

---

[1] Matthew 22:36-40 (paraphrased); Romans 12:9-10.
[2] Example; similar, but not the same.

Scriptures to Live By

Psalm 1

¹ **Blessed is the man that walketh not in the counsel of the ungodly, nor standeth in the way of sinners, nor sitteth in the seat of the scornful.**

² **But his delight is in the law of the Lord; and in his law doth he meditate day and night.**

³ **And he shall be like a tree planted by the rivers of water, that bringeth forth its fruit in its season; its leaf also shall not wither; and whatsoever he doeth shall prosper.**

⁴ **The ungodly are not so, but are like the chaff which the wind driveth away.**

⁵ **Therefore, the ungodly shall not stand in the judgment, nor sinners in the congregation of the righteous.**

⁶ **For the Lord knoweth the way of the righteous; but the way of the ungodly shall perish.**

Joshua 1:9

⁹ Be strong and of a good courage; be not afraid, neither be thou dismayed: for the Lord thy God is with thee whithersoever thou goest.

Psalm 32:8

⁸ I will instruct thee and teach thee in the way which thou shalt go; I will guide thee with mine eye.

Psalms 84:11

¹¹ For the Lord God is a sun and shield; the Lord will give grace and glory. No good thing will he withhold from them that walk uprightly.

Proverbs 3: 5 and 6

⁵ Trust in the Lord with all thine heart; and lean not unto thine own understanding.
⁶ In all thy ways acknowledge him, and he shall direct thy paths.

Isaiah 26:3

³ Thou wilt keep him in perfect peace, whose mind is stayed on thee: because he trusteth in thee.

Romans 12:1 and 2 (in part)

¹ ...Present your bodies a living sacrifice, holy, acceptable unto God, which is your reasonable service.
² And be not conformed to this world, but be ye transformed...that ye may prove what is that good, and acceptable, and perfect, will of God.

Philippians 4:6 and 19

⁶ **Be anxious for nothing, but in everything, by prayer and supplication with thanksgiving, let your requests be made known unto God….**

¹⁹ **But my God shall supply all your needs according to his riches in glory by Christ Jesus.**

James 4:4(b)

⁴ **… whosoever therefore will be a friend of the world is the enemy of God.**

James 4:7 and 8 (a)

⁷ **Submit yourselves therefore to God. Resist the devil, and he will flee from you.**
⁸ **Draw nigh to God, and he will draw nigh to you.**

James 5:16 (b)

¹⁶ **The effectual, fervent prayer of a righteous man availeth much.**

I John 4:4 (b)

⁴ **Ye are of God, little children, … greater is he that is in you, than he that is in the world.**

I John 5:14

¹⁴ **And this is the confidence we have in him, that, if we ask anything according to his will, he heareth us.**

Revelation 3:5 and 6 (in part)

⁵ **...I will not blot out his name out of the book of life, but I will confess his name before my Father, and before his angels.**
⁶ **He that hath an ear, let him hear....**

The Great Commission

Matthew 28:19-20

"Go ye therefore, and teach all nations, baptizing them in the name of the Father, and of the Son, and of the Holy Ghost:

"Teaching them to observe all things whatsoever I have commanded you: and lo, I am with you always, even unto the end of the age. **Amen.**"

The Whole Armor of God[1]

Believers, put on God's whole armor --
Like warriors -- everyday ...
Before you walk out in the world ...
To protect and guide your way.

It defends against the devil,
His wiles, and fiery darts;
Against darkened principalities;
Evil powers, and wicked hearts.

Gird your body in the **Truth of God**;
Put on the **Breastplate of Righteousness**.
Put on the shoes of the **Gospel Peace**;
Grasp the **Shield of Faith** to combat all wickedness.
Put on the **Helmet of Salvation**;
Grasp the **Spirit's Sword: God's Word**.
Then with **Prayer and Supplication**[2],
Let The Gospel News be heard!

---

[1] Ephesians 6:10-18.
[2] Thanksgiving.

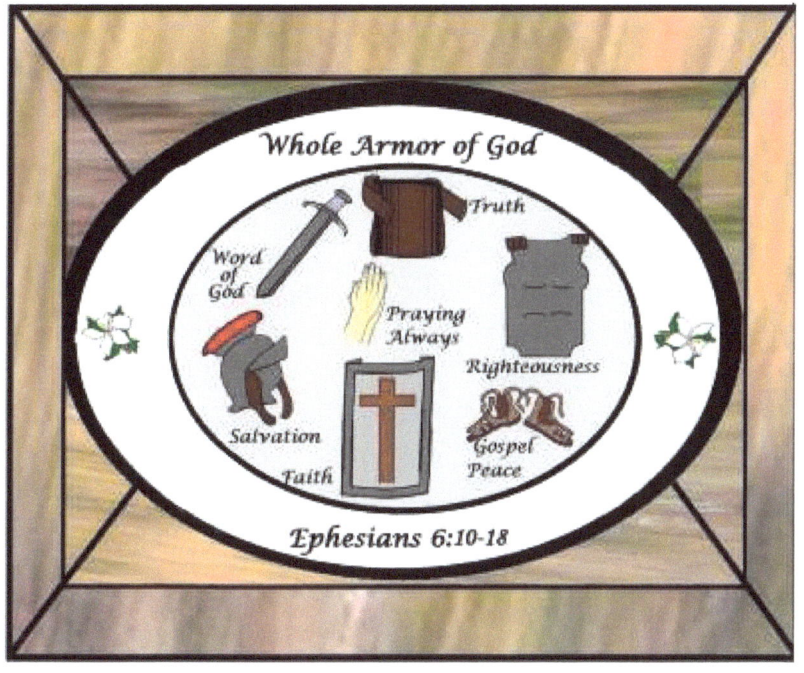

Singing Hymns and Gospel Songs

All soldiers marching into war
Need songs of victory and praise.
Singing hymns within your heart -
Keeps thoughts on God and spirits raised!

The hymns of old recall the truths
Of faith, salvation, and God's power;
In times of troubles and temptations …
How we "Need Thee Every Hour."

"In the Garden," "O, Glorious Day!"
"Near the Cross," "Trust and Obey";
"Amazing Grace," "A Thankful Heart,"
"Rock of Ages," "How Great Thou Art!"

Sing with gusto! With conviction!
Sing the hymns of saints in heaven.
They will comfort and inspire;
Praising God for all He's given!.

The J.O.Y. of Salvation

No matter what your calling ...
To business, service, ministry ...
Within Christ's wheelhouse is a map
It should not be a mystery.

Pick up your cross and follow Jesus;
Give of yourself, as He has said.
Put Jesus first and others second;
To peace and joy, you will be led.

God Will Lead You

God has a plan and a purpose
Meant for you ... it is His best.
He planted it within your being;
He will guide you. You need not guess.
If you take the time to listen
For the wee, soft voice within,
It will keep you on God's pathway ...
Lead to God's glory ... away from sin.

Keep Jesus Christ in your subconscious;
Think on Scripture when you rest;
When your mind and thoughts are drifting,
Don't let the world construct a nest.

You will hear the voice of Jesus ...
It is soft, but it is strong.
You will learn to love and trust it ...
It will never lead you wrong.
If you'll trust it and obey it,
Leave to God the consequence,
You need not ever fret or worry ...
God will be your strong defense.

Progressing on Your Christian Journey

Along the way, you'll hit some walls --
It's only human to back-slide.
But God is ready to forgive you;
Your every need, He will provide.

He'll give wisdom, if you study
Proverbs, Ecclesiastes, more...
The Psalms, The Gospels, Paul's Epistles...
Eternal truths...please, don't ignore.

A tip: don't try to read the Bible
In one year ... that's much too fast.
Read with reverence ... as God intended;
Eat[1] and drink[2] it... as God's repast.[3]

God will reveal His plan ... your purpose
Unique ... designed for you alone.
In His way is life fulfilling,
And by its trials, you will be honed.

With focused study of the Bible
And prayer time every day,
The fruit of works will be developed:
Your love for Christ be on display.
Growing a relationship
With the Trinity ...
Sowing seeds[4] for Jesus ...
Reaping for eternity...
In these, you'll know God's blessings ...
Abundant and pouring out.
They'll bring glory to the Savior...
'Tis the mature Believer's route.

[1] Jeremiah 15:16
[2] John 4:14
[3] Nourishment.
[4] Mark 4:3-20.

Colossians 1:9-14

Notes

Notes